OVER-EVERYTHING ABOUT PARENTING

30 DAYS TO A BETTER RELATIONSHIP WITH YOUR CHILD

By Josh Brandon

A Part of the

Your Journal Journeys

Series

First published by Josh Brandon Media, 2024

Your Journal Journey copyright © 2021 by Josh Brandon
Overthinking Everything copyright © 2018 by Josh Brandon
Josh Brandon Media appreciates your support in purchasing a legal edition of this book and for complying with any and all copyright laws by not reproducing, scanning, or distributing any part of this book in any form without permission. By doing so, you are supporting writers of all levels everywhere.
ISBN: 979-8-9884778-9-1
Artwork by yindeeicons, goodstudio, Giuseppe Ramos Designs, sketchify, Pbig, NotionPic (www.Canva.com)
Book written and designed by Josh Brandon

thanks for your support

Josh Brandon

ACKNOWLEDGEMENTS

Children are our greatest asset to ensure and establish our future. I want to acknowledge the educators and the parents, grandparents, support system, and the many villages involved with raising a child. It is difficult and heart wrenching while joyful and purposeful. Creating better people living amongst other people is the most important task and duty we have in life.

I acknowledge those who step up and seek to connect authentically with their child in a meaningful way to affect positive change in their lives.
I want to acknowledge the parents who try very hard to 'get it right' and may we one day figure what that looks like.

I want to acknowledge the stepparents who take on a blended family and loving another person's child as their own.

I want to acknowledge the grandparents, aunts, uncles, and cousins who help raise children and those who take in other people's children. We can never underestimate life's traumas that may impact our children, but we can work hard to be better examples for our children, and I hope this book and series helps us be more mindful of the ways we can affect even small change in a person's life.

DEDICATIONS

This book comes from trial and error. I wasn't that guy who wanted a family. I never wanted to have kids. But having them has been the greatest joy in my life. Having children changed me and I love this version of me so much more than I ever could have the man I was before. For Tori, Emily, Maddie, and Sara, I wasn't always the best father or father figure, and I dwell on my mistakes because just like my podcast, I'm *Overthinking Everything*. Still, I rejoice in the splendor of the successes while trying to learn as best I could from my shortcomings and failures. Each of you brought me different lessons and a love I never knew I needed so much.

To my girls, you are loved and always will be. In writing this book, I looked back on our own experiences, and some of those I wish we'd shared. I thought of the ways I wish I had seen the world when you all were little and you inspired me to try and help other parents connect in authentic and meaningful ways with their children because I know that, in that, is the success of a child.

I love you with all my heart. I am so proud of the women you've become.

Thank you for letting me be your Dad.

DISCLOSURES

There is no guarantee offered for anything in this workbook or supplemental material.

The information presented herein represents the views of the author as of the date of this publication.

This book is for informational purposes only.

The author reserves the right to alter, update, or reconsider his opinion at any time.

The author, nor partners/affiliates, assume any responsibility for any omissions, errors, or inaccuracies.

Any reference to any person or business whether living or dead is purely coincidental.

The author is not a licensed or credentialed mental health expert.

Any and all advice regarding mental health, therapy, etc. is not professional or medical advice and should not be interpreted as such.

The author is not certified or credentialed in child or adult psychology, only the science and art of teaching.

The author is not a licensed or credentialed Certified Media Consultant. Any consulting of others, personal or professional, referenced herein is purely on an individual and independent basis.

MORE INFORMATION

mypodcastworkshop.com

JoshBrandonMedia.com

OverthinkingEverythingPodcast.com

INTRODUCTION

This journal is designed to provide some insight and deep thought into yourself and your relationship with your child. These prompts and activities are intended to infuse fun into your week and open you up to different ideas and perspectives, as well as to explore a deeper, more meaningful, and authentic bond with your child.

Parenting is hard and often thankless. Children rarely realize what parents put into their relationships. Few parents are trained in the psychology and human development science involved with how to connect with their child as they grow and mature.

As parents, caregivers, or guardians, we do the best we can. We can all strive for a closer bond with our child. Resources like this help. Wisdom, Memories, and Time are the greatest gifts a parent can give to their child. Thank you for investing this time in your child. Please reach out to me on social media and let me know how this journal worked for you!

Happy Parenting!

WHY THIS IS SO IMPORTANT TO ME

    My journey as a parent has been filled with highs and lows, like you. However, as a child of divorce, the last thing I wanted was to continue the generational trauma cycle. Unfortunately, my first marriage ended, and my daughter's mother was a less-than-cooperative coparent. In fact, after my father passed away in 2007, I began to see the drama and trauma I had surrounding me. I realized not only did I not avoid the self-fulfilling prophecy of generational trauma, I welcomed it - invited it in! I was working for very toxic, abusive bosses and coming home to a very toxic, abusive home. My children were suffering, and my mental health was suffering.

    Stepping away from all that cost me greatly. My marriage ended with my children being taken from Georgia back to Tennessee without my consent. We had just moved, so I didn't have anyone I could call for help, not even a lawyer. While I was seeking an order to keep her from leaving with my daughters, she was halfway back to Tennessee. What followed was a contentious custody battle the likes you wouldn't believe. My relationship with my oldest two stepdaughters, forever altered. My relationship with my daughter held as some bargaining tool. In the end, I wouldn't give up. I fought through four lawyers, one corrupt judge, and an inept rural court system whose bias toward the mother despite all evidence, and thousands of dollars in expenses.

There I was, standing before a judge, begging to be a present father and that judge over and over denying me that opportunity, often postponing hearings, refusing to accept evidence, and content to allow my children, and me, to continue to be victims of abuse. The judge nor the courts were advocates for my children's rights or my own. My rights were violated, repeatedly, for years. But I wouldn't give up.

I wasn't making great money back then and driving home ten-plus hours to see my kids one weekend a month when gas prices were pushing five dollars a gallon was destructive to any rebuilding of my life I could do after divorce. Child support clipped me at the knees. Child support I was ordered to pay that was based off income *and* time spent with the child. Nearly $1000 a month of my earnings went toward child support and trips to see and spend time with my children. I couldn't even afford a lawyer to fight for my rights.

Eventually, I found a lawyer who took my case because he saw how I had been mistreated by the court. He made it his mission to get my daughter back for me. He got the ball rolling and most importantly, he got my case reassigned to the county where I lived, which was more evolved where family court issues were concerned. After several of the hardest years of my life, I would win what I should have never had to have fought for in the first place. The court and my attorneys said my case was a travesty of justice. That did little to console my broken heart or replace the time and memories I lost as a parent. That admission is no consolation prize for the mental abuse and anguish we all suffered at the hands of that judge and their mother, that we all still deal with in therapy today.

Everyone loves a happy ending, right!?

I have one!

What came from it was an appreciation for fatherhood - a perspective many don't experience. I learned to value quality over quantity. I took whatever time I could get with my children, and I made sure to make it count! Even if money was tight, and we had to hang out at my grandmother's house all weekend, we would play board games, watch movies, and try to make every moment special.
When my case ended and I was awarded my just-due parental rights, I committed then and there that my life was going to be about special moments, connecting with my daughter, making up for lost time, and making sure she and all my daughters were OK. Back during the custody battle, when it was just me and my biological daughter, when we were just getting Sundays together, my stepdaughters weren't allowed to come, since the judge couldn't order that

since, as their mother pointed out, I had no legal rights to a relationship with the girls who called me "Dad". In those Sundays, just me and Maddie, I would take her to do all the things I wish we could do together normally. We would go to Dollywood, or roller skating (which was a disaster), or to the movies or mall. I would love taking her to the mall as a child and watching her eyes light up at all the stuff she was interested in! We would go out to eat and go to parks and play and sometimes we would have picnics!

    These are memories that most parents take for granted or never get to experience because of the stressors, time, and financial constraints of life. I came to see that while I was coping with lost time and trying to cram every memory I could into a Sunday afternoon, I was also making a great effort to make my child feel loved, wanted, and seen. I had to be aware of the entitlement and "spoiling" my daughter, which is a legitimate concern that comes with its own mental health challenges for everyone involved.

    Fortunately, my daughter wasn't as adversely affected from our adventures as she was the abuse we all fought so hard to survive. Today, I look at my girls, all dealing with their respective challenges, but thriving and dealing with their issues, like their dad. I want to help other parents connect with their children in healthy ways, to form strong bonds with their children that will stand adversity and the test of time.

WHY THIS IS SO IMPORTANT TO YOU

This series is written through experience but also from a scientific standpoint. Specifically, the philosophy behind Your Journal Journey was inspired by the science of habit. These books and the goals they help you reach are inspired by groundbreaking habit-forming science designed to help you not only get into the habit of positive change, but commit to it for a more permanent change to your life.

There are many trends on the internet or social media of challenges that inspire the consumer of that content to affect some sort of change. When I considered this, it was just a straight-forward journal, with not much else. Once I began researching why this was so important to me, I began understanding that I should share some of what I learned with you because it will help you in your parenting journey. Let's understand a little better about how habits, good and bad, are formed.

DOWN THE HABIT HOLE

Habit formation is something many researchers (and advertising executives) have explored for many years. According to Charles Duhigg's *The Power of Habit* (2012), there is something called the *habit loop*, which ties into brain science and how our body's natural neurological pathways work. The habit loop is the philosophy behind forming habits and it's based on repetition to deepen and strengthen new neural pathways that can help us achieve our goals.

Think of it like pioneers out on the trail. That trail takes time and a lot of wagons going down that specific space of land for that land to form an actual wagon trail. The grass needs to be worn down, eventually off, to make those two dirt trails we're so used to seeing in old western movies.

Our brains are very similar, according to Duhigg's research. It takes time and repetition to wear that trail for our neuropathways to travel down. Another great metaphor for this would be like digging a ditch to reroute water! The water will go the way the water flows, same as with information in our brain. We must train the water – the information – the wagons, where to go!

The biological term for this is **neuroplasticity**, which refers to the brain's power to rewire itself, relearning new ways for even the brain to work. When looking at the daily activities, we are reinforcing new neural pathways that prioritize child-centered thinking and parenting. The more we do them, the stronger those pathways – and the results – will become. Eventually, they're our new normal!

The habit loop in Duhigg's book is broken down into three parts:

Cue: We need some kind of command to signal to our brain it's time to go into autopilot! Like hypnosis, we are tapping into our subconscious with cheat codes! We are hacking our brain's root directory!

Routine: This is what we do after the cue. This is the work behind the habit we are working on. This needs to be structured and consistent to work best.

Reward: Our brains need that positive reinforcement that drives repetition. Your dog expects a treat after doing a trick, your brain is the same in this regard. Tell the brain, "Good brain!" and the brain responds positively, desiring more of that praise or reward.

Your Journal Journey is designed with the habit loop in mind, offering you the cue (dedicated critical thinking into your child as a person), the routine (activity focused on connecting with the child), and the reward (a stronger, more meaningful relationship). You will do this for 30-days with the guidance of this book. However, over time, as this process is repeated, your brain responds to the repetitive cycle, rewiring itself, digging those wagon wheels in deeper, making the behavior natural and your default setting.

WHY 30 DAYS?

First, I wanted a full month's effort so that there is a more measurable result. This isn't to suggest every person who buys this book starts it on the first of a month, but in my mind, I thought that would be nice to take an entire month, dedicated to your child and how you would always look back on that specific month of that year as a turning point in the relationship. Those were my pipe dreams of helping others, not a guarantee of results, by the way.

Second, there is the idea behind the 21/90 Rule of habit-forming. The rule states that it takes 21 days to form a habit, and 90 days to turn that habit into a permanent lifestyle change. This is why so many people waste their money and time on a gym membership when what they needed was a dedicated 90-day accountability buddy! We can't go to the gym and take a day off then maybe go back.

We must commit to it for 90 days at least before the average brain says, "hey, this is normal now". And don't think you're so smart it won't take you that long. "Smart" people would have more challenges like thinking they knew better than the science so they would have to commit even longer to convince their very "smart" brain to rewire itself.

This isn't about intelligence. This is simply biological and how the brain works. This book encourages emotional intelligence and critical thought, but the science behind habit forming is not dependent on "smarts".

So, why 30 and not 21 or 90? Why not split the difference at least?

According to Dr. Phillippa Lally's 2009 study for the University College London it takes on average 66 days to solidify that habit into formation. I chose 30 to make the goal attainable for the reader, while not overwhelming parent and child, and leaving a clearer path forward for the parent to continue beyond the 30 days in this journal.

We want this to be a habit and habits take work. We must remember to focus on the routine, but also that cue and the reward because that, combined with 30- to-90 days of repetition, can affect permanent change.

A More Mindful Method

Through my book, **Overthinking Everything About You** and its companion **The Compassion and Critical Thinking Workbook**, I offer exercises and philosophy on recentering our brain for a more mindful and compassionate default setting. This is basically utilizing neuroplasticity to fuel the repetition and consistency of the routine in our habit loop.

However, the cue is deliberately forcing us out of our natural "all about me" default and into considering your child's perspective more. The routine is all about your child. The reward is a more understanding and compassionate parent so tuned into their emotional intelligence they more naturally have those bonding opportunities without having to deliberately create them.

Your child, above all else, wants you to be present, attentive, and active in their lives. Whatever it may seem on the outside, the science of child psychology doesn't lie. Children may sometimes act independent, but they are very much dependent on us – and they are biologically wired for that dependency – until we, or society weens them off it. We must hope we are present and attentive and active in their lives long enough for our influence to outweigh whatever makes them grow up too fast, like we did.

A 2017 study in the *Journal of Behavioral Health* found that mindfulness helps us become more self-aware, more aware of events around us, more aware of our own actions and the consequences of them.

That awareness leads to changing habits. This book encourages you to embrace mindful reflection on your own parent-child relationship, continuing to think critically, remaining engaged, and solidifying new habits and hopefully traditions for you and your child to bond over.

ACADEMIC CONFIDENCE AND THE "SMALL WINS"

I have discussed this in my other books, but it's relevant here, too. We all learn differently, and this book's activities might not be geared for your strengths. For that, I apologize. I hope one day to create this in a more multimedia format for all learners, but for now, writing is the best way I know how to express thought. What I know from my education and experience is that not everyone is a writer, and that anxiety related to trying to write for someone who isn't natural at writing is relatable to me because, while I *am* a writer and most of the time it flows freely, I also have many other things that terrify me, if asked to try.

Academic Confidence is the educational philosophy that if you feel good doing something you'll do better than if you feel bad doing it. So, grading systems that are strict pass/fail and don't encourage retries actually do more harm than good in many cases.

A grade is just what someone else thinks you know based on a sometimes science-based, but usually non-nuanced scoring system. However, to the student, a 73 isn't a great grade and it is discouraging (or sometimes fuels determination to do better). Whereas, incorporating a retry on the assignment provides practical real-life skills. Think of it as turning in a project at work and it gets sent back to your desk to correct a few things before it gets sent back out to everyone else. You learn on this task and for future tasks, as well. You aren't hindered by those mistakes, and it doesn't impede your progress. You learn more in the process.

We aren't looking to be passed when we aren't hitting our benchmarks in school. It's about setting realistic, attainable goals specific to the learner to obtain the *"small wins"* we need to push us to do more. This is the reward in the habit loop. Psychologist BJ Fogg wrote about *"small wins"*, in his 2020 work Tiny Habits, that, through *"small wins"*, we build momentum that drives us toward lasting and impactful change.

Each day of this journey, you will experience the reward - the small win - of connecting with your child in a way maybe you hadn't before. These shared memories, moments, and conversations between you and your child, if continued in deliberate, daily fashion, can affect the kind of life-long change you hope for.

THE LOST GENERATION OF COVID KIDS AND DIGITAL DISTRACTIONS

Another idea I've discussed in other books is the generation of children who had at least four years of their development impacted by the COVID-19 Pandemic. We will be studying, researching, and learning about the impacts of that event on our children for generations to come, I'm afraid. While many tried to do their best in an unpredictable situation, without laying blame anywhere specific, some serious weaknesses in our society and specifically our education system were exposed.

> "The COVID-19 pandemic has had profound effects on child development, exacerbating inequalities in access to education, mental health services, and social interactions. Prolonged school closures have contributed to learning loss and emotional strain on both children and parents." - Dr. Dimitri Christakis, *Journal of the American Medical Association (JAMA) Pediatrics* in 2020.

When we look at the years 2019-2024, in our society, we must account for the learning gaps experienced in that pandemic. We must accept that the experience of children, whatever phase of learning, was disrupted and corrupted by an event we cannot quantify.

That is why it is more important than ever that we take the time for deliberate reflection on our relationship with our children. They are exposed to so much more today than any generation before. Children are given access to information younger and younger, and the trauma connected with online bullying or worse is immeasurable. This is why it is important to you and your child's emotional and mental well-being to form as close a bond as possible because they are going to need you in their lives more than we needed our parents.

> "Excessive screen time is linked to a range of negative mental health outcomes for children including anxiety, depression, and sleep problems. The effects are compounded by the lack of face-to-face interaction, which is critical for healthy emotional development." – Jean Twenge, *iGen: Why Today's Super-Connected Kids Are Growing Up Less Rebellious, More Tolerant, Less Happy – and Completely Unprepared for Adulthood*, 2017.

While some of the interaction encouraged in this book is media-based, it is to learn more about your child's interests. The idea behind this book is to interact with your child intentionally face-to-face. Twenge's warnings are real, and her title is apropos. When we think of children growing up, especially post-pandemic, we can see some of the impact of that experience – the trauma of it – coming back to haunt us in the future.

> "Many parents struggle to spend time with their children due to competing demands, such as work schedules, household responsibilities, and financial stress. This often leads to feelings of guilt and inadequacy, which can affect the quality of the time they do spend together." – Sara Harkness, *Parents' Cultural Belief Systems: Their Origins, Expressions, and Consequences*, 2009.

This is why the activities in this book are actionable, manageable, and child-centered, designed to fit into your schedule. This book and the habits we're trying to form are intended to help alleviate that parental guilt we all feel by focusing on intentional moments of connection with purpose, no matter what life throws at us.

> "Children bond best with parents when their interactions are aligned with the child's interests and hobbies. Engaging in shared play helps establish a secure attachment and strengthens emotional bonds." – Dr. Lawrence Cohen, *Playful Parenting*, 2001.

The philosophy behind this book is earnest, genuine, and heartfelt. I want to encourage more parents not to give up on their child just because they've entered a certain phase of their life, when connecting with them seems harder. While this specific journey is geared more toward preteen and older, you may adapt this as you see fit for any age child.

The most important thing is to bond with your child in a way that is focused on the child and not 'all about me' as a parent. Too often we seek to relate to them, but we try to through ourselves when we should be trying to relate to them through their perspective and experience, adapting to their world as they see it, so they will "let us in", and put their guard down. Even as parents, we must constantly build trust. Children today have hurt and negativity coming at them from every angle. It is our job, as parents, caregivers, or guardians, to ensure that child is protected from those outside influences as well as our own unresolved trauma.

    This book is primarily designed to help you through helping them. I hope you get to know your child better through this process. Even more, I hope you get to know yourself better, too.

How It Works

It is encouraged to journal at a consistent time, usually at the end of the day as you unwind and reflect. Many of the writing prompts are set as challenges, activities, or exercises that might encourage you to talk to your child about a topic and then write about the conversation. In these cases, at the bottom of some pages, you will be given homework for future exercises. This is why it is important to follow the workbook for 30-consecutive days.

Your homework assignment will be in preparation for the next day's task or one shortly after. If you are supposed to write about it or do something, your homework will give you the info you need for the next prompt. I mean, you could just turn the page but who likes spoilers?!

Life happens and schedules are crazy. If you have an activity as your journal entry for that day, but life doesn't allow for that to happen, simply bookmark that day, schedule that (as most of us have to), and then pick up where you left off after that entry. It is best to stick to 30 CONSECUTIVE days, but if you miss one here or there, simply pick up where you left off – and journal about the detour!

On the first page, you will write a letter to your child. This is a free-writing exercise where you will write your feelings to your child. Your homework will be at the end of each day's first page, with a free page to continue your writing to follow. I have designed this book so that each day's pages are on the same page as you open the book, for your convenience.

TIP: Use sticky notes or a multi-colored pen to make additional notes in the margins!

If you choose to download the accompanying file, so that you can save this as a digital document, save that to a cloud and print it out once complete, so you always have a backup.

At the end of this, you will have one final writing assignment to recap everything you've learned and experienced. Please share with your child your honesty and authenticity.

Whether or not they ever see this is up to you. You may choose to buy the book and do it as a joint activity with your child or you may choose to buy the book as an experiment to help guide you through bonding activities. I encourage open and transparent discussions with children, but you may find it beneficial to get more genuine responses or reactions than if your child is internally thinking, "oh, this must be from that corny book".

However you approach this, Your Journal Journey is designed to be gifted to your child after, as an eternal reminder of your love and honest feelings. Your child will forever have a lasting keepsake of your earnest and unconditional love they can turn to and pass on to their own children.

Memories last a lifetime.
Documented memories last generations.

DAY 1 — Write a letter to your child. Tell them something you wish you knew when you were their age.

HOMEWORK: Engage your child in a conversation. It can be about anything but pay close attention to what they tell you and save it for later.

Continue Writing on the Next Page

DAY 2

Write about two things you learned about your child or their interests while listening in conversation today.

HOMEWORK: Pick a task for you and your child to do together. Something that won't take long and is more fun or creative than cleaning or chores. Play 5 Questions: Rules are you can't ask something you aren't willing to answer yourself; and they can't be revealing or prying questions. (Remember, we want to get to know our child, not interrogate them!

Continue Writing on the Next Page

Keep Writing!

DAY 3

Regarding your homework task from Day 2, write about the experience with the game 5 Questions. What did you learn about your child? What did they learn about you? What do you hope they will take away from it?

Continue Writing on the Next Page

Keep Writing!

DAY 4

Pick one thing you do well, as a parent, and write about where that quality or trait comes from in your life, why that is important to you, and why you feel it is important to your child.

HOMEWORK: Engage your child in a conversation about their future, but do not pressure them. Ask about their dreams and goals and what they want out of life.

Continue Writing on the Next Page

Keep Writing!

DAY 5

You were to have a conversation with your child about their dreams, goals, and what they want out of life. What did you discover about your child? Did you learn anything new? Can you identify common ground with your own goals and dreams at that age?

Continue Writing on the Next Page

DAY 6

Regrets aren't worth dwelling on, but let's dig one up for this exercise. What is something you regret in life that you hope can be a life-lesson imparted to your child?

Continue Writing on the Next Page

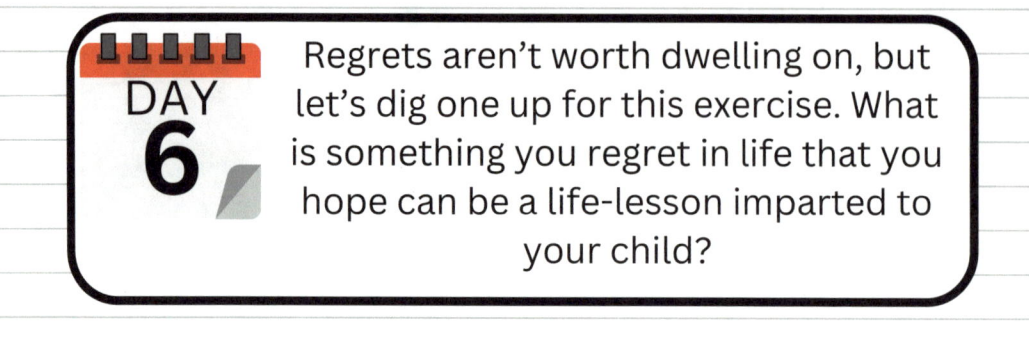

Keep Writing!

DAY 7

Find a top trending TikTok or social media video. Try to "hop on the bandwagon". Surprise your child by sending them a funny video based on a top trending TikTok or social media trend. DO NOT POST IT ONLINE. Just send it to your child privately. If they want to post it, let them.

Continue Writing on the Next Page

Keep Writing!

DAY 8

What is something from your childhood that you have seen reflected in your child's life?

HOMEWORK: Ask your child to play their favorite song. Listen to it without commenting or interrupting, but reacting positively (even if it's not your favorite)

Continue Writing on the Next Page

DAY 9 — Write about what you learned listening to your child's favorite song.

HOMEWORK: You are going to ask you child about their favorite social media influencer/celebrity, what they like about that person.

Continue Writing on the Next Page

Keep Writing!

DAY 10

Who is your child's favorite social media influencer or celebrity? What did you learn about your child from this conversation?

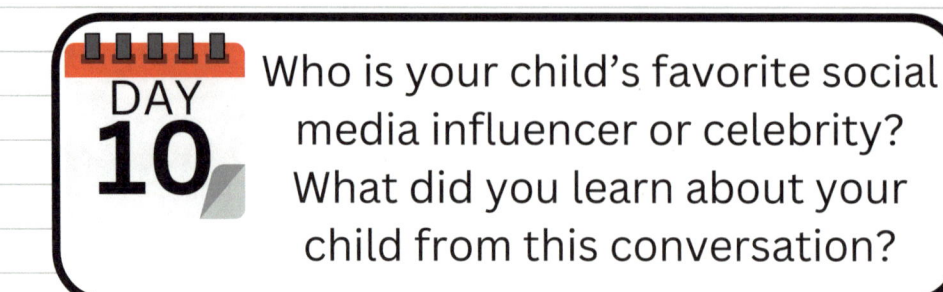

Keep Writing!

DAY 11

Write about specific gifts you have gotten your child that have meant something to you.

Keep Writing!

DAY 12

What is something about your child that you admire? Where do you think that trait comes from?

HOMEWORK: Engage your child in a conversation. It can be about anything but pay close attention to what they tell you and save it for later.

Continue Writing on the Next Page

DAY 13

Write about the most memorable vacation experience you have shared with your child. What would you do differently?

Continue Writing on the Next Page

Keep Writing!

DAY 14

What is an activity you and your child enjoyed when they were younger that created a memory for both of you? How might you update that for today?

HOMEWORK: Update that idea and recreate it for you and your child to do tomorrow!

Continue Writing on the Next Page

Keep Writing!

DAY 15 — Write about the previous day's activity. Did anything surprise you? What did you enjoy? Was there anything you'd do differently?

Continue Writing on the Next Page

Keep Writing!

DAY 16

What is something about your child's style that sets them apart or helps them fit in? How does their style compare to your own when you were that age?

Continue Writing on the Next Page

Keep Writing!

DAY 17

What are some things your child struggles with? How do you think you could better support your child in these challenges?

Continue Writing on the Next Page

Keep Writing!

DAY 18

Write about an experience you wish you could do over as a parent. What is your "...if I knew then what I know now..."?

HOMEWORK: Set aside 30 minutes tomorrow and think about a critical life lesson you can teach them about in an interesting way.

Continue Writing on the Next Page

DAY 19

Whip out the check books, scrub that cast iron with salt, and pour soda down the drainpipe, it's time to teach your child a life hack, life lesson, or practical skill that they will need as an adult. Write about the skill you want to teach. Find out more from your child. Start by asking them if there is anything they are curious about or want to know that they do not. They might surprise you!

Keep Writing!

DAY 20

Write about something your child is passionate about that you just don't understand. This could be a current fad, trend, dance, game, etc. Does this compare with something from your own childhood that your parents didn't understand?

HOMEWORK: Ask your child to explain this thing they are passionate to you. Try relating your experience to them

Continue Writing on the Next Page

Keep Writing!

DAY 21

What did you learn about your child from talking to them about the things they are interested in? What common ground did you find?

Continue Writing on the Next Page

Keep Writing!

DAY 22

What is your favorite photo of you and your child? Write about that memory and what it means to you. What do you think it means to your child?

HOMEWORK: Find your favorite photo of you and your child from when they were younger. Recreate it and, if you're comfortable, share with your close friends and family on social media using #journaljournies.

Continue Writing on the Next Page

Keep Writing!

DAY 23

Describe your ideal one-on-one getaway with your child? What foods would you eat? What activities would you do? Where would you go?

HOMEWORK

As your child their dream vacation and listen carefully. Allow them to open up. Feel free to share your own dream vacation ideas with them.

Continue Writing on the Next Page

Keep Writing!

DAY 24

What did you learn about your child though talking about your dream vacations?

Continue Writing on the Next Page

Keep Writing!

DAY 25

Your child knows something you do not know. Today, you were to ask them to tell you 5 things they think THEY know that you do not! Let your child be your teacher today. Write about what you learned. What do you think about the things they chose?

Continue Writing on the Next Page

Keep Writing!

DAY 26

Immediately before you child was brought into life what were your greatest fears or anxieties as a parent? How have those fears been eased as your child has grown?

Continue Writing on the Next Page

Keep Writing!

DAY 27

This one's kind of dark. Imagine you've been gone/dead for 10 years. Write about what you think your family will say about you after you're gone. How do you hope they will describe you to future generations and others as they tell stories of you?

Continue Writing on the Next Page

Keep Writing!

DAY 28

Remember yesterday? Imagine you've been gone for 10 years. This time, write about what your family WILL say about you. Day 26 was what you HOPE they will say. It's time to get real with yourself. Is there a difference? Meditate on that, then write your thoughts.

HOMEWORK: Set aside a half hour and plan a quick meal with just you and your child. Make out ingredient lists and plan a shopping trip to grab what you need!

Continue Writing on the Next Page

Keep Writing!

DAY 29

CAR PICNIC!

Ask your child where they want to eat. Hit the drive-thru and find a spot you both enjoy and do a spur of the moment picnic. Use it as an opportunity to connect with your child. Ask your child how they feel about your relationship after the last few weeks. Write about what you learned.

Continue Writing on the Next Page

Keep Writing!

DAY 30

YOU MADE IT! *(Almost)*
We began this journal with an open letter to your child. Given the last 29 days, write another letter to your child.
(Ideas might include how your ideas or perspective on them or your relationship have changed.)

Continue Writing on the Next Page

Keep Writing!

> **HOMEWORK:** You've connected over food in the car, on-the-go. Now let's connect in the kitchen by preparing and cooking the meal you planned together and enjoying it with love.

WRAP UP

Write about your experience and how this helped you grow as a parent, what you learned, what surprised you, and what memories you will cherish from this experience. Tell them to your child, in hopes that this will one day give them inspiration and comfort for when they want to pursue a better relationship with their child.

Continue Writing on the Next Page

Keep Writing!

CONGRATULATIONS!

YOU DID IT!

HOMEWORK

Learn from what you learned here and use that to enjoy a stronger, closer, and better relationship with your child! Please share this journal series with others you know who would benefit.

Conclusion

I hope you grew a fraction from this book as I grew writing it for you. I hope you enjoy a more mindful approach to parenting, closer connections with your child, and better bonding experiences. Parenting is a work in progress, and we are all fighting for the same goal – to raise good humans who are good to others.

Remember the lessons learned here and the valuable information to apply to your perspective, especially the science of habit forming. I think affecting any great change in our lives requires hacking into our brain's mainframe, so to speak, rewiring those neural pathways to create new pathways that work better for us and create better outcomes.

Please share your experience with this book online and with friends and family.

There's more to learn about social media and podcasting in my book **INFLUENCE!**
I want to invite you to explore the possibilities of sharing your story through podcasting.
My Podcast Workshop is a talent coaching workshop that focuses on the most important aspect of creating content or podcasting –
YOU!

MYPODCASTWORKSHOP.COM

Please visit the website to learn more.
Do more than just Create...

INFLUENCE!

Do not forget that there are additional materials available to help you along your journey and even more related materials, updates, and more on my website at:

ABOUT THE AUTHOR

Josh Brandon is a voice actor, performer for film, television, commercial and stage, a public speaker and public speaking instructor, as well as a social media content creator, podcaster, and activist.

He is the host of the podcast *Overthinking Everything* and author of the book series inspired by it, including *Overthinking Everything About You*, *The Compassion and Critical Thinking Workbook*, as well as *INFLUENCE,* and the *Your Journal Journey Series.*

As a talent coach with media personality experience spanning three decades, Josh Brandon is the founder of *My Podcast Workshop,* bringing his diverse knowledge to social media content creators seeking to grow their brand beyond a single platform.

For more information on Josh Brandon, please visit:

JOSH·BRANDON MEDIA.COM

EXTRA PAGES IF YOU NEED THEM
Keep Writing!

DAY

Keep Writing!

DAY

Keep Writing!

DAY

COMING SOON

WITH YOUR SUPPORT

More from the Your Journal Journey Series

---

30 Days to Being a Better Partner

30 Days to Being a Better Dad

30 Days to Being a Better Man

30 Days to Being a Better Boss

30 Days to a Better Realtionship with Your Parent

30 Days to Being a More Compassionate Person

Made in the USA
Columbia, SC
08 February 2025